Clam Digging & Crabbing in

Oregon

*an informative guide on
clam digging and crabbing
in Oregon.*

by John A. Johnson

Table of Contents

DEDICATION

As a youth my brother was always my hero. He was a star athlete in high school, a brave Marine on two combat tours in Viet Nam, and now a great adventurer in the last frontier. To be like my brother was my childhood goal and it remains so today. Thanks Stan for everything.

Clamming & Crabbing
in
Oregon

Copyright 1990, John A. Johnson
P.O. Box 1601
Waldport, Oregon 97394

ISBN 0-937861-10-3

First Printing, June 1990
Second Printing, June 1990
Third Printing, June 1991
Fourth Printing, June 1993
Fifth Printing, June 1995
Sixth Printing, April 1999

ADVENTURE NORTH PUBLISHING CO.

P.O. Box 1601, Waldport, OR 97394

Printed by
Wegferd Publications
North Bend, OR USA

John A. Johnson

Acknowledgements

I wish to thank my wife Shirley for hours of tedious typing and helpful suggestions.

Many thanks to Tom Gaummer and Darrel Demory. Clams and crabs are their respective professions with the Oregon Department of Fish and Wildlife and they are the best. Without their support and editorial comments this book could not have happened.

Lieutenant Commander James S. Dicks, U.S. Coast Guard, provided most aerial photographs of the Oregon bays and for this I am very grateful.

My father, Stanley, provided the idea and encouragement to write this book.

Jason Campbell contributed several of the cover photos.

Finally a special thanks to my high school classmate and friend Mari Van Dyke. Her maps and realistic drawings added a special touch to this book.

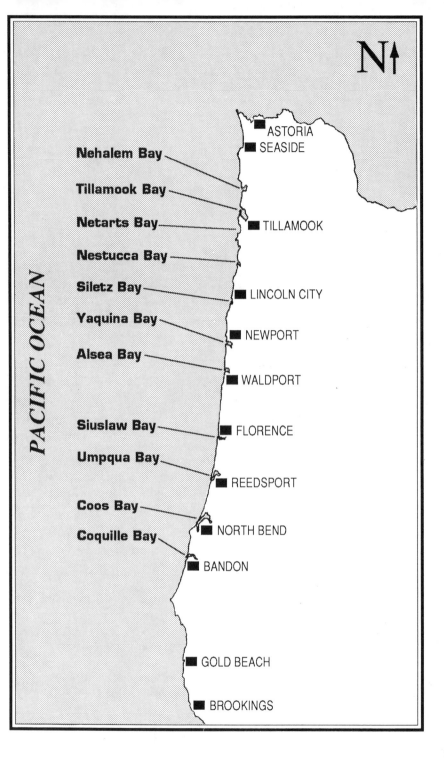

N

PACIFIC OCEAN

Nehalem Bay

Tillamook Bay

Netarts Bay

Nestucca Bay

Siletz Bay

Yaquina Bay

Alsea Bay

Siuslaw Bay

Umpqua Bay

Coos Bay

Coquille Bay

ASTORIA
SEASIDE

TILLAMOOK

LINCOLN CITY

NEWPORT

WALDPORT

FLORENCE

REEDSPORT

NORTH BEND

BANDON

GOLD BEACH

BROOKINGS

INTRODUCTION

I grew up along the northern Oregon Coast digging razor clams at Seaside, exploring tidepools and mussel beds near Cannon Beach, and crabbing with my parents, brother and sisters on picturesque Nehalem Bay. This bonding between myself and the natural resources of the Oregon Coast grew stronger after six years as a commercial clam digger which aided in my economic struggle through college.

My education and occupation pulled me inland for several years where I missed the roar of waves, smell of fresh salt air and those ever present opportunities to enjoy the quality recreation on the Oregon Coast. I live again on the Oregon Coast and hope never to leave it.

It is my desire by writing this book on clam digging and crabbing in Oregon to open the eyes of some Oregon residents and coastal travelers to the truely unique outdoor experiences available at "the beach". In addition to good family-oriented outdoor fun, this book will guide the seafood gourmet to unlimited seafood delights.

In your pursuit of clams and crabs please remember, take only what you need, obey regulations, and don't litter. Let's preserve what we have so future generations can enjoy Oregon's gift to all.

BUTTER

SOFTSHELL

LITTLENECK

GAPER

COCKLE

photo courtesy of ODFW

Shells from the five species of bay clams most commonly dug in Oregon estuaries.

Stan and Margaret Johnson

CLAM DIGGING IN OREGON

"Wake up lazy, it's a beautiful morning and there's not a cloud in the sky. Is there any way I could talk you into digging us a batch of clams?" My wife Shirley never seems to get her fill of clams.

"OK," I said with a yawn. "What kind do you want today?"

"Surprise me," was all she said.

I left my house in Reedsport at 7:15 am and was heading down the road toward the Umpqua Bay when I realized I needed to decide what kind of clams I wanted to dig. If I hurried I could drive through Gardiner and out 3-Mile Road for a chance at razor clams near the North Jetty. I could boat down-bay to "The Point" where I had always dug limits of half-pound softshells. I finally decided to try for the giant gapers I'd been hearing about. They were rumored to be found by the old Coast Guard pier in Winchester Bay.

A minus 1.5 tide exposed a large mud-flat about as much as I'd ever seen it. I approached to find the remains of several large holes obviously dug last tide. A couple of 13 pounds with my shovel handle and there was no doubt I had found the spot. Large black holes nearly an inch across mysteriously appeared as the huge necks retracted from the surface. I picked out one hole and began to dig. I touched the tip of the neck about a foot down and finally reached the huge shell down another foot. I stuck my thumb in the gape along side of the thick leathery neck and tried to pull it up. No such luck. Another ten minutes and one very tired arm and I was holding the largest clam I'd ever seen. It easily weighed over two pounds! Another hour and I was heading home with six clams and enough tasty seafood to feed the entire family.

As I drove home all wet, cold and tired, I thought about how fortunate I was to live in such an area. Here in the lower Umpqua Bay I could dig for three species of clams. Within a short half-hour drive I could be in Coos Bay digging for five species of clams or go north of Florence and gather mussels growing thick on kelp-covered intertidal rocks. Anyone who lives on or visits the Oregon Coast can do the same. By boat, car, or foot, you are never far from excellent clam digging, superb seafood tablefare, and a truely unique and unforgettable Oregon outdoor experience.

Razor clam digging in the "surf" can be real sport - they rapidly dig down to escape when disturbed.

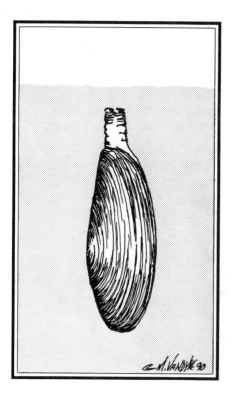

THE
RAZOR
CLAM
(Siliqua Patula)

The shining jewel among Oregon's many miles of wind swept beaches and bleached white sand is the razor clam. It is the best known and most widely sought clam species in Oregon. The reasons for this are as varied as the sport diggers I have interviewed. Most agree that the razor clam is the best eating of all bivalves in Oregon or the entire west coast for that matter. They are usually dug along the picturesque beaches of northern Oregon in clean sand that is free of rocks and debris. Many will tell you that digging razor clams is truely a sporting experience and a real challenge. They are the only Oregon clam species that upon being disturbed will rapidly dig deeper to avoid capture. Another reason may be that a razor clam is relatively easy to clean and yields a high percentage of edible meat. No matter what the reason, the razor clam is truely king among Oregon's clam species and unquestionably my own personal favorite.

The razor is found from Alaska to northern California. In Oregon an 18 mile stretch of sandy beach in Clatsop County between the mouth of the Columbia River and Seaside is where the bulk of the razor clam population thrives. However, isolated small populations of these knife-edged shellfish are found along the entire Oregon Coast. Fair numbers of razor clams have been located in Tillamook and Coos Bay and on the beaches near Newport, Reedsport, and Gold Beach on the south coast. No population level, however, compares to those found near Seaside.

30
Many people believe the razor is the best eating of all Oregon clams.

The razor clam's scientific name, *Siliqua patula*, literally means spreading foot which refers to the muscular foot or digger. Razors dig by combining water with muscle action to spread this "foot" and pull the body downward into the sand. The thin oval-shaped shell covered with a smooth brown glossy covering reduces resistance. These features combined with a powerful digger, allows the clam to pull itself downward rapidly. A razor clam can dig up to nine inches a minute in soft sand. Vertical movement is common but horizontal movement from one location to another has never been observed.

Razors spawn in late spring or early summer at two years of age or older. Eggs and sperm are broadcast in the ocean when water temperatures reach 55 degrees F. Young clams grow fast and reach one inch in a few weeks and three to four inches in one year. Oregon razor clams live to four to five years of age and measure six inches in length. An eight-year old clam is considered a real grandpa!

A stainless steel clam shovel is expensive but well worth the cost.

Low tide allows the digger to approach the clam where he lives. How low is the question. A minus tide is considered best because the lower margins of the beach is where the greatest concentrations of clams are found. Generally speaking, a one-foot minus tide or better provides the best digging opportunity. I have, however, dug limits of razors at Seaside on a + .5 low tide when ocean conditions were very calm.

Calm ocean conditions are an important consideration when digging razor clams. Rough surf retards feeding activity and also makes it difficult to see the bottom when digging in the water. A rough ocean can also be a real safety hazard. More than one razor clam digger has lost his life during such conditions. A good rule of thumb is to dig one and one half hour before a low tide until one hour after low tide. Tide books can be purchased at most sport shops and hardware stores along the coast.

TOOLS AND EQUIPMENT

Any narrow-bladed shovel which allows the digger to extract a wedge of sand from the surface will do. I prefer a straight blade, five inches wide by eight inches long with a slight "cup" to it. Custom clam shovels made of stainless steel are available in the Seaside/Astoria area but they are expensive!

Some diggers prefer using a "clam gun" which is a metal tube two feet long and five inches in diameter. It has a handle and is open at one end. It is inserted over the clam hole and when extracted, a column of sand is removed, and hopefully, also the clam.

Any porus container can be used to carry around your catch. If you can attach it to your belt, all the better. A small burlap or nylon mesh sack is great.

Good hip boots are a must and chest waders even better. A wet clam digger is an unhappy clam digger.

HOW TO DIG

There are basically two methods of digging razors, in the water and in the "dry" sand. Most beginners will dig in the "dry" (actually quite wet) sand as it is easy to find the "show" or dimple left after a disturbed clam pulls its neck in and begins to dig down. The depression is usually 1/4 to 1/2 inch in size. Stomping on the sand with your feet or shovel will usually cause a clam to "show". A razor clam will be found anywhere from six inches to three feet beneath the surface. They always dig down at an angle toward the ocean. A clammer must dig on the ocean side to intercept the clam as it digs to escape. Only experience will tell you just how far away from the "show" to dig, but a good rule of thumb is about six inches. Most experienced razor clammers prefer the sport of digging in the water. Wade out into a foot or so of water and pound with your shovel handle when the water is clear enough to see the bottom. A disturbed clam will show a puff of sand or a depression about 1/2-inch in diameter as it pulls its neck down and begins to dig away. Experience and speed are the ingredients for successful razor digging. You'll feel a real sense of accomplishment when you sack your first limit of razors while digging in the surf.

PREPARATION FOR THE TABLE

Cleaning a razor clam is relatively simple. First separate the animal and shell. A sharp, thin-bladed knife can be used to slide down each side of the shell cutting the round paired abductor muscles. The whole clam can now be easily removed from the shell.

A much easier and less messy procedure is to simply drop the clams into boiling water a few short seconds, until the shells pop open. Now, immediately place the clams into cold water so as not to overcook them. The meat and shell will easily separate. It should be emphasized that boiling the clams too long will overcook the meat and ruin the flavor and texture of the meat.

Now you are ready to clean the clam. With a knife, separate the neck or siphon and the foot. Cut the brown tip off the neck and split it lengthwise. Split the foot lengthwise and scrape out all dark colored organs. Wash the meat thoroughly and it is ready to be cooked.

COOKING

Razors may be battered and fried whole, cooked as fritters, or made into clam chowder. The best way to ruin a good batch of fried clams is to overcook them. Cook for 30 seconds at 350° on each side in a well-greased pan and better seafood you won't find!

Kai, my daughter, with a nice mess of razors.

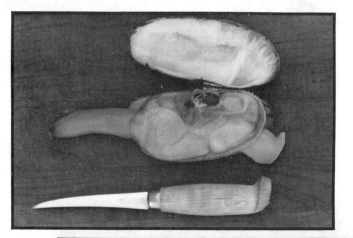

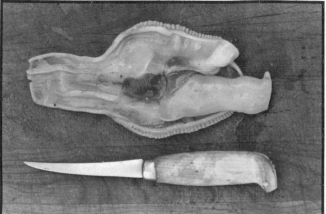

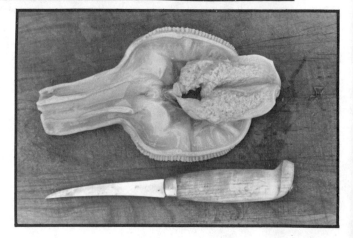

How a razor clam is cleaned. Other clams can be cleaned in a similar manner once they are out of the shell.

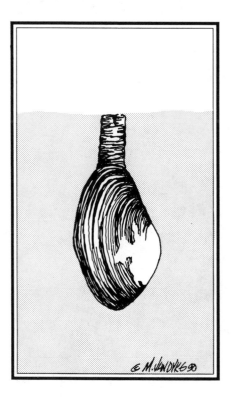

GAPER
CLAM

(Tresus capax)

The gaper clam has a variety of common names depending on where you are on the Oregon Coast. Around Coos Bay it is called the Empire Clam and in the Tillamook area it is known as the blue or blue neck because of the blue color of the meat near the tip of the neck. In many locations along the coast it is called the horse clam or horseneck because of its large neck. It is most often called the gaper clam because of the opening or gape at the posterior end of the shell.

Whatever you choose to call it, the gaper clam is the largest clam found in Oregon. A mature clam will have a shell five or six inches in length, four to five inches in height and weigh up to five pounds. The total weight of the dressed clam meat ranges from 15 to 35 percent depending on the season. One big gaper will feed a normal person nicely but be sure to pound the tough neck before cooking or get ready for cramps in your jaw muscles.

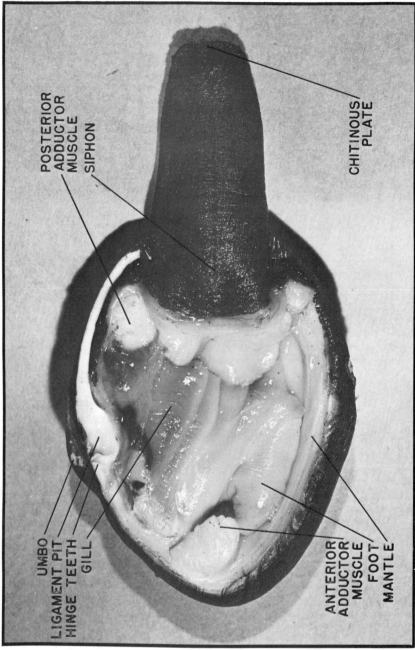

POSTERIOR ADDUCTOR MUSCLE

SIPHON

CHITINOUS PLATE

UMBO

LIGAMENT PIT

HINGE TEETH

GILL

ANTERIOR ADDUCTOR MUSCLE

FOOT

MANTLE

photo courtesy of ODFW

This is a gaper clam, however, other clams look basically the same when the shell is removed.

Gaper clams can get quite large. This clam weighs nearly three pounds. A few of these and you've got a meal.

Gapers live in a mud-sand substrate type and are found in most of the larger bays. They inhabit the lower flats and channels of the bays and most are found below the 1.0 minus tide line. A minus tide or better is usually necessary to have successful gaper digging. It is common in Tillamook, Netarts, Yaquina, and Coos bays.

The presence of gaper clams is revealed upon disturbance of the surface by walking or pounding. Gapers are found from 12 to 18 inches beneath the surface of the mudflat extending the tip of the neck to the surface to feed. Unlike razor clams, the gaper does not dig down after being disturbed, but remains stationary its entire life. When disturbed, the huge neck is pulled down revealing a large hole one inch or greater in size. The tip of its neck can often be seen but is usually camouflaged with its brown skin flaps or thickly attached algae. The suction felt by probing a suspected clam hole with your finger is a dead give away that you have found a gaper.

Now the work begins. More physical effort is required to capture this clam than any other. A good shovel with a wide blade is a necessity. Dig rapidly or the mud or sand comes in quickly. When you reach the clam, it is often awkward to bring it to the surface because it is difficult to grip. A secret I've learned is to stick my thumb in the gape next to the neck and pull slowly with the thumb and forefinger. Don't try to retrieve the clam by gripping the neck — it will inevitably break and you'll lose the clam.

A proven method used by knowledgeable diggers is to cut out the bottom of a five-gallon bucket, placing it down over the clam hole as you dig. Work it down as you dig and this will prevent collapse and allow you to retrieve the clam with much less effort.

Gaper clam diggers usually need a good minus tide for best results.

Jason Campbell with an average-sized gaper.

PREPARATION FOR THE TABLE

Cleaning —

To clean a gaper, the procedure is very similar to cleaning a razor clam with one exception. A thick leathery skin covers the large neck of a gaper and can be very difficult to remove. Separate the neck and the foot. Soak the neck in near boiling water for about three minutes or freeze the necks overnight and the tough skin can easily be removed.

Cooking —

Gapers have a flavor second only to razor clams in my opinion. They can be fried in batter, made into fritters, or they make excellent chowder. The neck of a gaper is as tough as leather and must be tenderized by thorough pounding. A single fried neck from one of these huge clams will nearly fill an average dinner plate.

(Photo by Jason Campbell)

Dan Campbell uses a section of a metal pipe to help him reach a deep gaper clam.

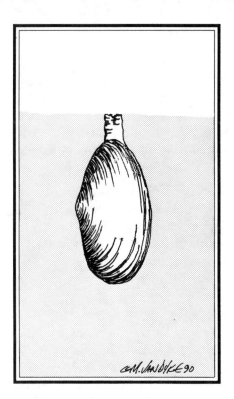

THE
SOFTSHELL
CLAM
(Mya arenaria)

The softshell clam is a native of the eastern seaboard and was transplanted to the west coast in late 1800s. This clam is commonly called the eastern softshell, steamer, or mud clam.

It is a medium-sized clam ranging four to six inches in length and 1/4 to 1/2 pound in weight at maturity. This oval-shaped clam usually has a chalky white brittle shell that is extremely sharp. This is no doubt how it acquired its most common name - softshell. Cut fingers are a common occurence among the softshell diggers and many use rubber gloves to prevent this problem.

Like the gaper clam, softshell clams have a very long neck that allows them to live six to twenty inches beneath the surface. It extends the tip of the neck to the surface to feed, extracting food organisms from the water. The softshell is similar to the gaper clam in that it can retract its long neck but the body remains stationary and invisible in the mud.

They do not dig away to escape. Mud clams are common in most Oregon bays and usually abundant in the upper reaches of the larger estuaries. They prefer a muddy substrate but I have dug hundreds of softshells in the sand. Although some softshells live below the tide line (subtidally), most are intertidal. A minus tide is not necessary to reach them, any good low tide is usually sufficient to expose their beds.

Very little sport harvest occurs in most bays with the exception of the Umpqua, Siuslaw, Yaquina, and Coos bays. The Umpqua bay is generally recognized as having the best habitat, population, and largest average size softshells in Oregon.

HOW TO DIG

Softshell clams are detected by an oblong hole up to 3/4 inch in diameter, but is sometimes hard to see in soft mud. You can often feel the neck retract by sticking your finger in the hole. Ghost shrimp (sand shrimp) and softshells frequently live in the same area and surface holes look similar. Beneath the surface ghost shrimp create a maze of tunnels going all different directions whereas a clam hole is always vertical.

Any good garden shovel will do for digging softshells. There are basically two ways to dig softshells: dig individual holes or find a good concentration of clams and simply dig a trench about two feet deep and pluck the clams as they are exposed.

To dig mud clams individually, start digging slightly off to one side so as not to crush the clam with the shovel. When you find the clam (six to twenty inches down), gently grasp the whole shell and pull it out being careful not to cut your fingers. Don't try to pull up a softshell by the neck as it will usually break off.

Softshell digging is a messy sport at best. It is smart to wear a pair of waders and rain gear top and bottom. These bivalves are not called mud clams because they generally live in clean white sand!

Dig one large hole when softshells are numerous.

Umpqua Bay may have the best softshell clam population in the state.

35

PREPARATION FOR THE TABLE

Cleaning

Small softshells make excellent steamer clams and can be eaten whole when so prepared. In fact, softshells are commonly called steamers on the east coast as this is how they are most often eaten. Be sure and soak the clams for at least 12 hours in clean cool water and they will pump their systems clean.

Large softshells are best cleaned by first soaking them in near boiling water for about three minutes. This pops the shell open and allows the clam to be pulled free or easily cut from the shell. It also makes the easy removal of the clear slim coating that covers the neck. Now follow the same procedure used to clean razor and gaper clams.

Eastern softshells have excellent flavor quite similar to that of razors. They can be fried whole, ground up for fritters, or used in clam chowder.

Extremely low tides are not necessary for good softshell digging.

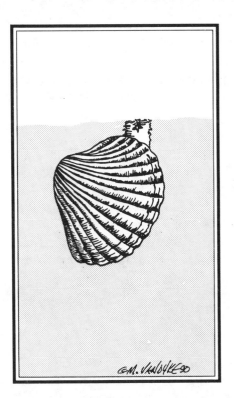

G.M. VANDYKE 80

THE
COCKLE
CLAM
(Clinocardium nuttalli)

The cockle is a two to four inch clam that can be easily identified by its many prominent and evenly spaced ridges on the exterior of the shell. Other names for the cockle are basket cockle and cockerel. Its color will vary from a light brown when found in sand to a darker gray when the habitat is muddy.

The cockle is found in most bays of Oregon and is one of the most popular clams in terms of recreational harvest. It will be found in the sand flats of the lower bay areas. It is most common in Tillamook, Netarts, Yaquina, and Coos bays.

The cockle has a very short neck and therefore is found only one to three inches beneath the surface and has limited lateral mobility. The hole is difficult to detect, sometimes showing up as a small double hole less than 1/2-inch total length.

A rake is the best and most common way to gather cockles. A standard garden rake with three-inch tines does a great job. Should the holes be readily visible as they are on rare occasions, a shovel works well for digging individual clams.

Cockles are most often eaten as steamers, in clam chowder, and some folks will also fry them whole. In any case, leave the clams over night in clean salt water and allow them to pump themselves free of sand. Cleaning is accomplished by steaming or dropping the clams directly into boiling water until the shells pop open in a few short seconds. Further cleaning of the clam is unnecessary. Dip these clams into melted butter and lemon juice and the taste is heaven.

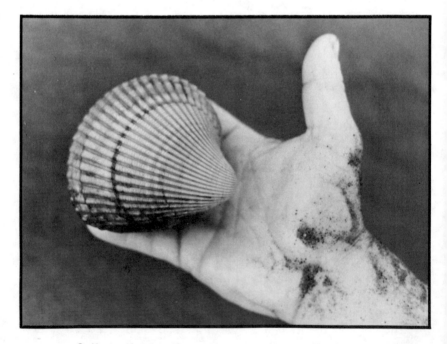

Cockles are a fairly large clam and make excellent clam chowder or fritters.

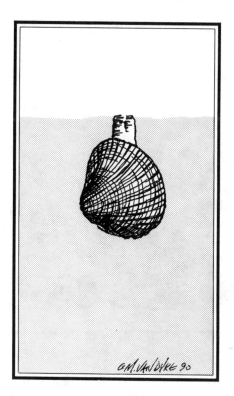

GM.VANDYKE 90

THE LITTLENECK

(Venerupis staminea)

The littleneck clam is quite small and averages only about two to three inches in size. Also called steamers, butter and rock clams, it is similar in appearance to the cockle in that the radiating ribs are visible, but they are much less prominent.

The littleneck is found in limited sand and gravel areas of larger bays and gravelly ocean outcroppings. It is heavily dug in Tillamook and Coos bays. It is found from one to six inches beneath the surface and is often picked up incidentally while raking for cockles. Their hole is shaped like a figure-8 and is 1/4 to 1/2 inch long. In areas of heavy concentrations it is dug by turning over the substrate with a fork or shovel.

Littlenecks are the clams you get when you order steamers in restaurants and are most often prepared that way. They make superb tablefare when dipped in a mixture of melted butter and lemon juice after steaming them open. Like cockles, they should be left overnight in clean salt water so they will pump themselves free of sand.

Littlenecks or steamer clams are small but superb tablefare when steamed and dipped in melted butter and lemon sauce.

Littleneck clams are normally found low in the bay and in a sandy substrate. A long-tined rake is the best way to gather steamers.

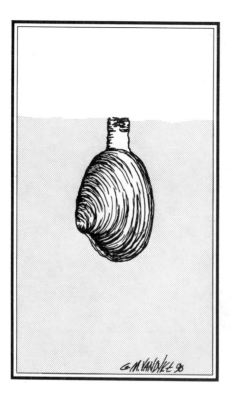

THE
BUTTER
CLAM
(Saxidomus giganteus)

The butter clam is also called the Martha Washington clam, Coney Island, quahog, or beef-steak clam because of its pink colored meat. It is identified by its two to four-inch heavy ovate shell that shows fine concentric lines of growth on the exterior.

Oregon has relatively few beds of butter clams. This is due to lack of suitable habitat, a gravel-sand and mud mixture. They are found six to twelve inches beneath the surface and a long-tined rake, shovel, or potato fork is used to dig this species. The hole or "show" of this clam is cigar or figure-8-shaped and is 1/2 to 3/4 inch long.

The meat of a butter clam has excellent flavor and texture. They can be fried, used for chowder, or eaten as steamers.

A fairly large clam, the butter has a thick heavy shell and very tasty meat.

A clam digger raking for butter clams near Hobsonville Point in Tillamook Bay.

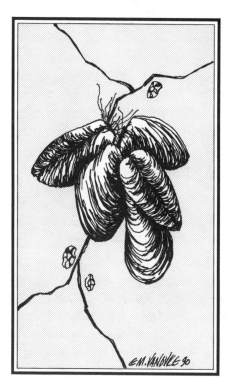

EM.VANDYKE 90

MUSSELS

Mussels are a coastal mollusk that inhabit the intertidal and subtidal areas along the Oregon coast. They live in clusters connected to the rocks or other solid objects by byssal threads which are secreted to form solid hold-downs. These byssal threads are often called the "beard" of a mussel.

Mussels, like oysters and clams, have long been one of modern and ancient man's favorite seafoods especially here in Oregon. The importance of mussels to the diet of coastal Oregon Indians can easily be observed by examining the remains of clam middens or shell piles found from the Oregon/California border north to the mouth of the Columbia River. In many locations they appear to represent the bulk of food items consumed while Indians inhabited these areas. When the tide was out their tables were set!

Mussels are still enjoyed around the world and are probably most famous in France where they are a prized delicacy. They are in such demand in Europe that tons of these black-shelled mollusks are raised each year through the practice of aquaculture farming. Here in Oregon, Roger Sardinia of Umpqua Aquaculture in Winchester Bay, is successfully culturing exotic mussels to fill the growing demand of gourmet restaurants throughout Oregon, California and Washington.

Two species of mussels commonly grow in Oregon waters. The blue or bay mussel (*Mytilus edulis*) is common to Oregon bays. It has a smooth blue-black or olive color to the shell and is about 2-1/2 inches long. The surf mussel (*Mytilus californianus*) is found along the rocky coastline in large beds and may reach a length of eleven inches.

The best time to sport-harvest mussels is during winter months when peak yields of meat occur although they can be gathered and eaten throughout the year. Users will find two to four-inch mussels collected from the lowest tide mark best eating. Harvesters should be aware that mussels are filter feeders and are subject to concentrations of saxitoxin causing paralytic shellfish poisoning. May through September is the time to be aware and public warnings are issued if danger is present.

The gathering of mussels is probably the easiest of all seafood quests. You find the mussels, put your hands on one, and give several twists which breaks the "beard" free of its attachment. A three-prong garden rake is also useful in this task. Gloves are definitely a good idea as the sharp shells can easily cut your fingers. Now, wash off the mussels and they are ready to steam open.

Any way you prepare a clam to eat, you can do the same for mussels. These edible mollusks eaten as steamers and dipped in seafood sauce are great. I have also enjoyed mussels deep fried in a thick batter.

Mussels are abundant along the entire Oregon coast. They are plentiful on most of the jettys and along much of the rocky ocean shorelines. Good mussel gathering areas include the following (from north south): Indian Beach and Cannon Beach, Lincoln City, Seal Rock, Yachats, Sunset Bay near Coos Bay, Bandon, Port Orford, and the Gold Beach/Brookings area.

Mussels that are 3-5 inches long are the best eating size.

Shirley Johnson with mussels gathered north of Florence.

SEASON – Open all year unless specified.
LICENSE – None required.

Species	Daily Catch Limit	Special Regulations
Clams Razor Clams‡	First 15 taken	‡Clatsop Co. beaches north of Tillamook Head closed to razor clam digging Jul 15-Aug 31.
		a. Unlawful to remove clams from the shell before leaving clamming area.
Bay Clams Butter, Littleneck, Cockle, and Gaper	20, of which only 12 may be gaper clams	b. Each digger must have own container, dig own clams and may not possess more than one limit of clams while in clamming area.
Softshell and others	First 36 taken	c Unbroken butter, cockle, or littleneck clams may be returned, but only in the immediate digging area; all other clams must be retained regardless of size or condition.

Be sure to consult the Oregon Department of Fish and Wildlife's fish synopsis for current regulations.

Clam digging is good family-oriented outdoor fun. (Photo courtesy ODFW)

CLAM CHOWDER

1 pound bacon, diced   6 cups clams, undrained and
1/2 pound ham, cubed   minced
4 cups chopped onion   7 cups milk
1/4 cup flour   Salt and pepper to taste
12 cups diced potatoes   Butter or margarine

Saute' the bacon and ham, drain off most of the bacon drippings, and save. Add the onion to bacon and ham mixture; saute' until the onion is limp. Stir in the flour. Pour enough bacon drippings back into the pan to fry the potatoes. Add the potatoes and fry, stirring constantly, about 15 minutes or until the potatoes are soft. Add the clams with liquid and cook 5 more minutes. Add milk; season with salt and pepper to taste. Dot with butter or margarine when serving.   SERVES 12-16

CLAM SAUCE FOR SPAGHETTI

1 pound spaghetti   2-3 tablespoons Parmesan cheese
3 Tablespoons butter   1/8 pound Cheddar cheese, grated
2/3 cup light cream   1 cup sauteed minced clams

Cook spaghetti; drain and return to pan. Reheat slowly and add remaining ingredients, one at a time, mixing well after each addition.   YIELD: 4-6 SERVINGS

CLAM DIP

1 8-ounce package cream cheese 1/4 teaspoon garlic salt
1 cup minced clams   1 tablespoon Worcestershire
     (sauteed')   Sauce
1 tablespoon mayonnaise   1/4 teaspoon monosodium
Crackers or chips   glutamate

Mix all ingredients in order listed. Use reserved clam juice to obtain the right consistency. Chill for 5-6 days before serving. Serve with crackers or chips   YIELD: 1-1/2 CUPS

47

FRITTERS

1 cup ground clams
1 cup corn meal
¼ cup flour
2 tsp. baking powder
1 egg
⅓ cup milk
⅓ cup or more of clam juice

Mix dry ingredients.
Beat eggs and add milk to it.
Add milk, egg and clams to dry ingredients and stir, adding enough clam juice to make a smooth thick batter. Fry by the spoonful in deep fat at 360° until browned. Drain on paper towel.

Serves 3to 4

COOS BAY OYSTER STEW

3 dz. lg. oysters in their own juices
1 tbsp dry, white wine, optional
1 cup black olives, sliced
2 tsp parsley, chopped
Dash of paprika

Dash of paprika
Salt, pepper

2 green peppers, chopped
2 15-1/2 oz. cans stewed seasoned tomatoes
2 tbsp. olive oil
1 anchovy fillet, chopped optional
2 tbsp croutons or seasoned breadcrumbs
Seasons to taste

Cook oysters in their own juices for a few minutes until firm (add a bit of water if necessary). Cut large oysters in bite-size pieces. Add canned, stewed tomatoes, the green pepper, oil and olives, as well as parsley and other seasonings. Cook over moderate heat, uncovered, for about 15 minutes for flavors to blend. Adjust seasonings, sprinkle a few croutons or seasoned breadcrumbs over each bowl. Servce with garlic bread. This recipe lends itself well to improvising and stretching. Cooked oysters can be added as needed as well as the other ingredients. SERVES 4-6

SPORT CRABBING

IN OREGON

Crabbing along Oregon's breathtaking coastline is a totally unqiue outdoor experience that you have to try to appreciate. Just imagine for a minute waking up early on a warm August morning, packing a picnic lunch for the whole family, and heading to the coast for a day of crabbing. You launch the boat and head out into the bay, dumping five or six baited crab rings over the side as you go. After an anxious 20 minutes you head for the bobbing floats and pull the rings up fast so the catch can't escape. The first pull reveals half dozen scrambling Dungeness crabs and two are keepers. Anxious and excited brothers and sisters compete to pull up each crab ring and soon there are enough crabs to head to the rocky shoreline and begin boiling the ocean-fresh salt water to cook the crabs. An hour later and a few more runs back to the center of the bay and there are plenty of tasty crabs to feed the entire family and enough left over for a crab salad back home.

By the time the day is over all the family members are ready for bed but anxious to return and do it all again. And why not? Fresh salty air, an inexpensive outdoor family adventure, and topped off with a meal of the finest seafood that Oregon has to offer.

A variety of crab species inhabit the Pacific Ocean and Oregon's many tidal bays, but, the Dungeness crab (*Cancer magister*) is what Oregon sport crabbing is all about. The Dungeness is mostly a deep-sea ocean dweller but good numbers of these one to three-pound crustaceans enter Oregon bays throughout the year. All Oregon bays have Dungeness crabs and many also have the red rock crab, a tasty but smaller and hard-shelled cousin of the Dungeness. The sheltered and less dangerous waters of these estuaries are where the majority of the sport harvest occurs.

Sport crabbers will catch two species of crabs in Oregon estuaries, the Dungeness (left) and the red rock crab (right).

Dungeness crabs start life as a free-swimming larval form called a megalops which are consumed by practically every fish species in the sea. By the end of their first year of life they have grown and shed several shells, a process called "molting". They shed their shells less frequently during their second and third years of life and reach full body size and weight by their fourth year. They often live to be 10 years old. The larger crabs most frequently "molt" in later summer and fall months and their shells are often soft at this time. Soft-shelled crabs have poor flavor and low meat content and should be released upon capture. Here in Oregon only male crabs that are 5-3/4 inches measured across the shell in front of the spines are legal.

Crabs are an opportunistic feeder and will eat practically any clam, fish, or other ocean organism they can catch or find. They prefer fresh food or bait.

Kids seem to enjoy crabbing as much as adults.

The most common equipment used for crabbing in Oregon bays are (left to right) the pot, ring, and folding crab trap. (Photo by Jason Campbell)

EQUIPMENT

Crab rings are the most frequently used type of harvest equipment here in Oregon. A small metal ring a foot or so in diameter forms the bottom and a larger metal ring 24 to 30 inches across is the top. They are joined by heavy fishing web or knotted mesh that covers the sides and bottom. A three-way rope is attached to the larger ring. A bright colored and highly visible float attached to the end of the rope helps the crabber locate his rings once they are set. A 50 foot length of rope is about right for most situations. Bait is secured to the bottom mesh. When the ring is lowered into the water the large ring and mesh collapse onto the smaller ring and the whole affair lays flat on the bottom. When sufficient time has passed and hopefully crabs are feeding on the bait, the ring is swiftly pulled to the surface and the crabs are caught in the funnel-like trap.

Crab rings are fairly inexpensive and work fine but they do have a couple of drawbacks. Most larger bays have good numbers of extremely intelligent harbor seals and sea lions that have learned to steal a free meal, namely your crab bait, from the open and unprotected crab rings. Traps and pots that protect the bait inside eliminate this problem. Another problem with rings is that crabs feeding on bait inside the ring are free to come and go. Frequent ring checks are necessary. Also, a swift and steady pull is required to keep crabs from escaping upon retrieval.

Crab pots are deadly crab catchers. They are simply two large metal rings separated a foot or so by bars and covered with wire mesh. They have one or two one-way entrances just large enough to allow crabs to enter but not escape. The advantages of crab pots over crab rings are that seals cannot steal your bait, entering crabs cannot easily escape, and frequent checks are unnecessary. Disadvantages are that they are heavy, quite bulky, and fairly expensive. Lose one of these and you will cry. Again, a good 50-foot section of rope and float are necessary.

The collapsable square metal crab trap is one of the most ingenious inventions to come along in years. They keep seals out, catch and hold crabs well, are less expensive and more available than pots, and they fold up for easy storage. In my opinion, these traps are the only way to go.

The folding crab trap is effective and folds up for easy storage.

There are several types of crab snares on the market but catch rates with these devices leaves something to be desired. Also, specialized garden rakes can be used to rake for crabs in "crab holes" left by the receding tide along the open beach line.

A good crab measuring device is a must. Currently only males that are 5-3/4 inches across the back are legal in Oregon. Measurers can be made or purchased from most sport shops along the coast and are much more convenient than a ruler or metal tape.

A large five-gallon kettle is a good idea if you intend to cook crabs yourself either on the beach or at home.

Good foul weather clothes and rubber knee boots are more than a good idea, they are essential. Coastal Oregon weather is unpredictable. Whether crabbing from a boat, dock, or pier, hope for sunny skies but be prepared for wet weather.

My daughter, Kai, enjoys crabbing.

The bait you use to lure crabs into your ring, pot, or trap can fill your boat with plenty of scrambling crabs or send you scrambling to the nearest seafood market to pay an arm and leg for a few not-so-fresh crab. Any fresh or frozen meat will attract crabs but some are better than others. Fish carcasses of any kind make excellent bait and a few sport shops carry frozen shad which I consider the ultimate crab bait. Fresh or frozen clams placed in bait containers also work very well. Good crab bait can be purchased from many outlets along the coast but remember, nothing is worse than running out of bait when these "sea spiders" are really thick. Bait size and type are an individual choice but be sure to secure it with wire or twine in the trap as current or crabs will carry it away.

Most Oregon bays have Dungeness crab populations and the larger bays have red rock crabs. With the exception of Netarts Bay, the amount of fresh water entering these estuaries from the rivers that feed them determine just how good the crabbing will be. Summer and fall months have the least rainfall and are the best time to crab. September and October are often the premium months for crab harvest.

All bays are affected by the tides and so are the feeding habits of the crabs. These critters are most active and easiest to catch when the tide is nearest to high or low slack tide. When the tidal current runs hard, either going in or out, this is when crabs bury themselves, don't feed, and wait for the water to slow down. Best time to crab is one hour before and after low or high tide. Crabbing also is good when there is little difference between high and low tide as this is when tidal currents are less severe. For example, try to pick a day when there is a **high** low tide and a **low** high tide. Under ideal conditions, this sport can be relatively good the entire 12-hour tide.

In general, the lower in the bay and closer to the ocean the better the crabbing will be. Also, a good rule of thumb to follow is that the more salt intrusion or penetration of ocean water into the bay that occurs, the better crabbing a bay will offer. For example, salt water moves up-bay much further in Coos Bay than it does in the Siuslaw and therefore Coos Bay consistently yields better crab catches.

Most bays have moorages where crabbing is allowed.

A lone sport crabber retrieves his crab ring from a pier in Coos Bay.

The most accepted method for cooking crabs is to boil them in salt water. Pure Pacific Ocean water has a salt content of 35 parts per thousand and that is ideally what should be used to cook crabs. If you are cooking your crabs at the beach, use water taken at near high tide and close to the mouth. Water used on the outgoing tide or from the upper bay will generally not have the desired salt content. When you cook crabs at home, add enough salt to the water to simulate the taste of ocean water.

Drop the crabs in the water once it has come to a full boil. Boil the crabs for a full 20 minutes, pull them from the water, and allow them to cool before cleaning.

The cleaning of crabs is really easy. Simply pull the back or shell away from the body and legs and then remove the feather-like gills and the yellow or orange organs. Most of the organs can be taken out with your fingers and the remainder can be washed out with water.

Removing crab meat from the shell is a messy business at best. I spread a thick layer of newspaper over the entire table and have at it. Only experience will determine the best way to get at the scrumptous meat but nutcrackers and a pointed utensil are very helpful. The flavor of fresh-caught crab meat is undescribably delicious and definitely well worth all the effort.

The meat of a crab is extremely perishable whether cooked or not and should be kept on ice if at all possible. Crab meat should be eaten within 24 hours if you do not intend to freeze it.

REGULATIONS

Regulations for crabs and crabbing are relatively few and straight forward:
- Crab season is open all year.
- No license is required for sport crabbing.
- The daily limit for Dungeness crab is 12 males per person that measure 5-3/4 inches across the back not including the spines.
- The limit for red rock crab is 24 per person per day with no size or sex restrictions.
- Each person is limited to the use of three rings, pots, or traps per day in any combination.

Be sure to consult the Oregon Department of Fish and Wildlife fishing synopsis for current and changing regulations. They are available free of charge at most sport shops.

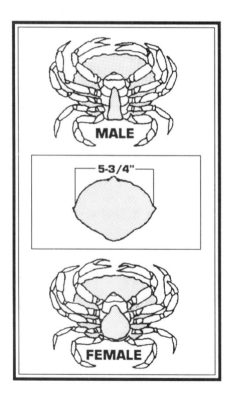

Many recipes are available for preparing and cooking crabs. Here are a selected few:

CRAB FRITTERS

1/2 pound crabmeat
2-1/2 tablespoons chopped onion
1 tablespoon chopped parsley
1 tablespoon chopped green pepper
2 tablespoons chopped ripe tomato

2 eggs
1 teaspoon Worchestershire sauce
1/4 cup flour
2 teaspoons baking powder
1/8 teaspoon salt
3 tablespoons butter
Lemon wedges

Thoroughly mix together the first 7 ingredients. Sift the flour, baking powder and salt into the first mixture. Stir until just blended. Fry by tablespoonfuls in hot butter over moderate-high heat, turning once to brown on both sides. Serve immediately accompanied by lemon wedges.   SERVES 4-6

ROLLS OF CRAB

1 pound American cheese, grated 3/4 pound crab meat
2-1/2 green peppers, chopped   1 cup tomato hot sauce
1/2 pint stuffed olives, chopped 48 rolls (poppy seed, hard or
1 cup butter melted   potato)

Combine ingredients and fill scooped-out rolls. Wrap individually in foil, twisting ends. Let stand in refrigerator overnight. When ready to use, put into covered pan and het 1/2 hour at 350°F.

BROILED CRAB SANDWICHES

1 6-ounce package cream cheese
softened
2 teaspoons lemon juice
1 cup flaked crabmeat
1 tablespoon chopped onion

1/2-1 teaspoon chili powder
to taste
1/8 teaspoon salt
2 tablespoons mayonnaise
4 split English muffins

Mix first 7 ingredients. Spread over English muffins; broil until browned.

CRAB CASSEROLE FOR FOUR

1 14-ounce can artichoke hearts,
drained
1 4-ounce can sliced mushrooms
drained
1 pound fresh or frozen crabmeat
drained
2 tablespoons butter
2-1/2 tablespoons four

1/2 teaspoon salt
Dash cayenne pepper
1 cup half and half
2 tablespoons sherry
2 tablespoons cereal crumbs
1 tablespoon grated Parmesan
cheese
Paprika

Cut artichoke hearts in half and place in well-greased shallow 1-1/2 quart casserole. Cover with mushrooms and crabmeat. Melt butter and blend in flour and seasonings. Add cream gradually and cook until thick, stirring constantly. Stir in sherry. Pour sauce over crabmeat. Combine crumbs and cheese; sprinkle over sauce. Sprinkle with paprika. Bake in hot 450°F oven for 12-15 minutes until bubbly.   SERVES 4

FETTUCCINE WITH CRAB

4 tablespoons butter
2 garlic cloves, minced
4 tablespoons flour
1/2 cup sherry or dry white wine
2 cups half and half

1/2 pound mushrooms, sliced
Butter
1/3 cup Parmesan cheese
salt and pepper
1-1/4 pound crabmeat
Cooked fettuccine

Melt 4 tablespoons butter in large skillet, add garlic and saute' until soft. Add flour and cook briefly. Gradually add sherry and half and half. Cook until sauce is smooth and thick; set aside. Saute' mushrooms in generous amount of butter. Add mushrooms and any juice to cream sauce. Stir in Parmesan cheese and add salt and
pepper to taste. Gently fold in crabmeat. Heat through. Serve over freshly cooked fettuccine, your own or store bought.
                                                   SERVES 6

SOUFFLE' OF CRAB

10 slices bread, crusts trimmed
3 cups crabmeat, tuna or shrimp
3/4 cup chopped celery
3/4 cup chopped onion
1/2 cup mayonnaise
1 cup chopped green pepper
4 eggs

3 cups milk
1/2 teaspoon salt (optional)
1 10½ ounce can cream of
mushroom soup, undiluted
Grate mild or sharp Cheddar
cheese
Paprika

Butter a 9x13 inch baking dish and line with half of bread slices. Mix together next 5 ingredients and put on top of bread slices in baking dishes. Top with remainder of bread slices. Beat together the eggs, milk and salt. Pour egg mixture over bread and refrigerate overnight. Next day bake at 325° for 15 minutes; removed from oven and spread undiluted soup over the top. Sprinkle with cheese and paprika. Return to oven and bake 1 hour longer. Allow to set 10-15 minutes before cutting.   SERVES 6-8

CRAB AND ARTICHOKE ELEGANTE

1/4 pound butter
3 tablespoons minced onion
1/2 cup flour
1 quart cream , heated to
boiling point
1/2 cup Madeira
Salt and pepper
2 tablespoons lemon juice
4 cups fresh crabmeat

3 9-ounce packages frozen
artichoke hearts, cooked
according to directions, or equal
amount canned artichoke hearts
6 ounces spaghetti or linquini,
cooked and drained
2 cups grated Gruyere or
Swiss cheese, divided
Paprika

Preheat oven to 350°F. Melt butter in large heavy pan. When butter sizzles, add onion and saute until golden. Stir in flour, cooking over low heat until flour is pale. Remove from heat. Add cream, stirring vigorously. Return to moderate heat and stir until sauce reaches a boil. Reduce heat and add Madeira. Season with salt and pepper; set aside. Pour lemon juice over crabmeat and toss lightly. Quarter artichoke hearts. Combine crab and artichoke hearts. Add cream sauce. Toss crab mixture with pasta and place in a 6-quart butter casserole. Stir in half of grated cheese. Sprinkle remaining cheese on top and dust with paprika. Bake 25-30 minutes, or until heated through.   SERVES 10-12

OREGON BAYS

Oregon bays, also called estuaries, are a unique environment where fresh and salt water meet forming a fish and wildlife habitat type found nowhere else on earth. Since time began man has been attracted to these coastal bays for both recreation and food gathering. We today are no different in that we still like to go to the bays for food and fun.

We are fortunate here in Oregon to have a large number of estuaries both large and small to fulfill our recreational needs. I have described the major estuaries in Oregon, excluding the Columbia River, where significant numbers of clams and crabs are available for public recreational harvest. I have tried to accurately describe where clams and crabs are found, numbers and locations of public access areas, and the amount of development that surrounds the bay. I hope this will help in selecting a site and planning your next coastal clam digging or crabbing experience.

After that last clam is dug or crab caught, take a little time to look around at the wildlife and scenery that surround you and think about the wonderful time you have enjoyed. Estuaries are extremely sensative and vulnerable to man's activities. Please take care not to harm Oregon's fragile few estuaries. These Oregon bays are Mother Nature's gift to all of us now and our children in the future.

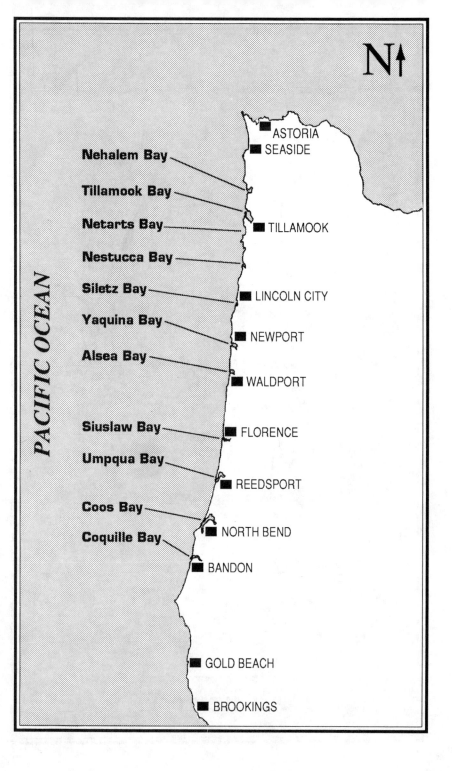

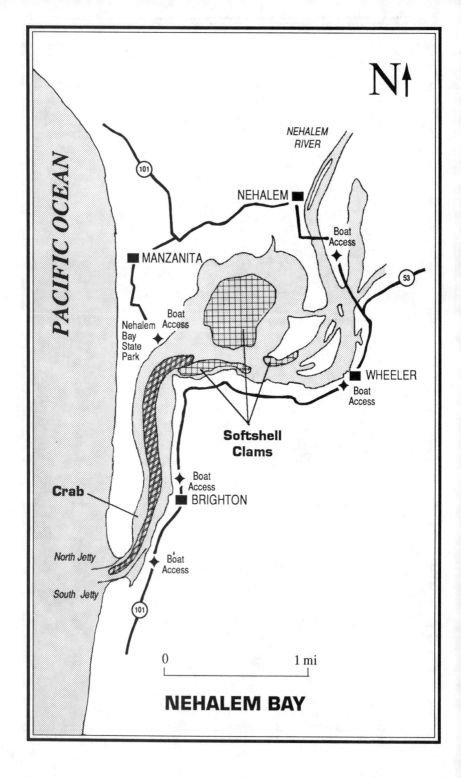

N

PACIFIC OCEAN

NEHALEM RIVER

NEHALEM ■

Boat Access

101

MANZANITA ■

53

Boat Access

Nehalem Bay State Park

Boat Access

WHEELER ■

Boat Access

Softshell Clams

Crab

Boat Access

BRIGHTON ■

North Jetty

Boat Access

South Jetty

101

0   1 mi

NEHALEM BAY

NEHALEM BAY

This scenic bay is the fourth largest in Oregon and unique in that very little development has occurred on and around it over the years. It is located south of Seaside about 20 miles along Highway 101 and is about a 1½ hour drive from Portland via Highways 26 or 53.

One of the best softshell clam beds in the state is located about three miles up-bay from the mouth and directly opposite the sleepy little town of Wheeler. This bed can be reached by vehicle off of the Bayside Gardens Road, however, boat access is the best way to go. Any minus or near minus low tide will expose these clam flats.

Crabbing is very good due to excellent salt water intrusion throughout the year. It can be quite good all year long, but late summer and fall seasons provide best catches. Crabbing is best in the main channel in the lower two miles of the bay.

There are several moorages along the bay where boats and crab rings can be rented and bait is available. Private and public boat access is no problem. At least two major campgrounds and several motels are located in the vicinity.

Nehalem Bay offers superb soft shell clam digging.

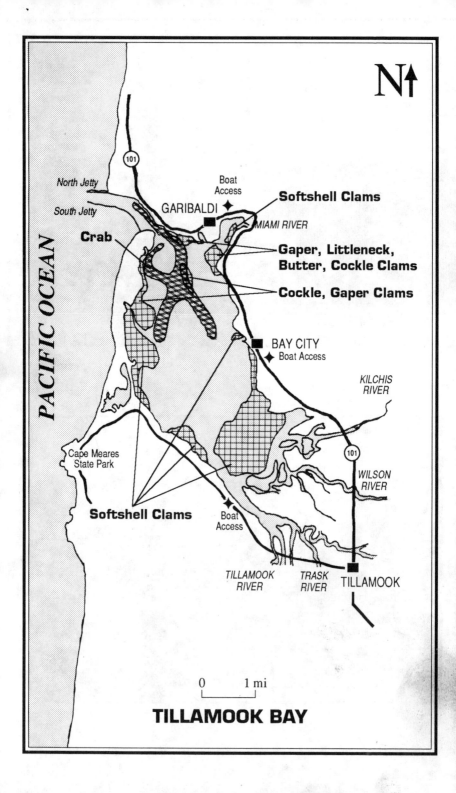

N

North Jetty

South Jetty

Boat
Access

Softshell Clams

GARIBALDI

MIAMI RIVER

Crab

**Gaper, Littleneck,
Butter, Cockle Clams**

Cockle, Gaper Clams

PACIFIC OCEAN

BAY CITY
Boat Access

*KILCHIS
RIVER*

Cape Meares
State Park

*WILSON
RIVER*

Softshell Clams

Boat
Access

*TILLAMOOK
RIVER*

*TRASK
RIVER*

TILLAMOOK

0   1 mi

TILLAMOOK BAY

TILLAMOOK BAY

Tillamook Bay is Oregon's second largest estuary and is located 70 miles south of Astoria along Highway 101. It is less than a two hour drive from downtown Portland via Highway 26. This huge bay has some of the best crabbing and clam digging that Oregon has to offer. Also, the largest artificially cultured oyster beds in Oregon are found here. These oysters, however, are privately owned and no public sport harvest is allowed.

Tillamook Bay supports a variety of clams but only five species are normally taken by sport diggers. A good population of softshell clams is found in the upper third of the bay. The average size is fairly small be they are quite plentiful. Bayocean Road on the west side of the bay provides the best access to this area. Goose Point near Bay City also has an excellent population of softshells. A plus .4 or lower tide is necessary to reach these clams.

The lower half of Tillamook Bay is home to the cockle, littleneck, butter clam, gapers and a few razors. Two of the best clam digging areas are Garibaldi Flat and the Hobsonville mudflat in the northeast corner of the bay. A small bed of large gapers is found on sand-flats just south of Crab Harbor near the Bayocean Peninsula. Digging large gapers in the luxury of rock-free sand is a pleasure indeed. Many good clam beds can be reached on foot but a boat will get you to more isolated clamming areas near the center of the lower bay. In general, a minus 1.3 or better tide is adequate to reach these beds.

Crabbing in Tillamook Bay is great and is done year round. Crabs move out into the ocean when the bay's five rivers flood the estuary with fresh water. Summer and fall are best crabbing seasons.

Crab rings, bait, and shovels can be bought or rented at several sport shops in Garibaldi and nearby Tillamook. Four boat ramps are located around the bay and plenty of motel rooms, restaurants, and campsites are situated in the area. Boat moorages and rentals are available in Garibaldi.

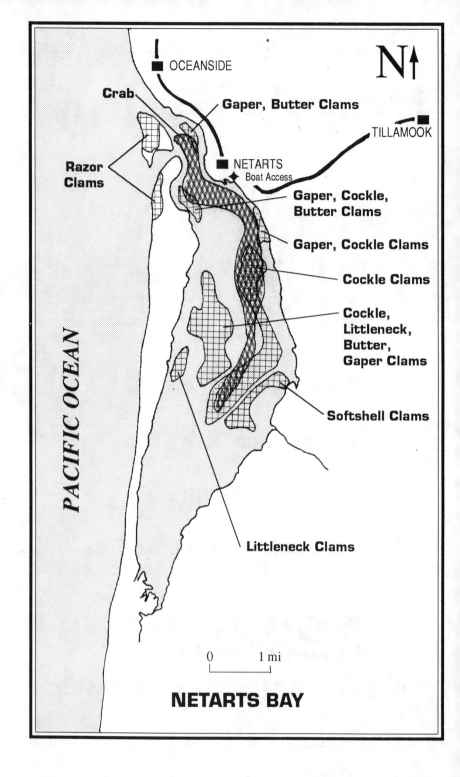

NETARTS BAY

NETARTS BAY

This mid-size Oregon bay is directly west from the town of Tillamook, only 1½ hours drive from the Willamette Valley and may well be one of Oregon's best kept secrets. It is essentially a saltwater bay fed only by a few small creeks. For this reason crabs can be taken here year-round since its ocean waters are influenced little by winter rains. This bay is quite picturesque with little development.

Clam digging is good for all species of bay clams which are found throughout this system and some razor clams are occasionally dug near the mouth. Digging for softshells is fair in the upper reaches of the bay. Happy Camp on the northeast shore near the mouth is a popular digging area and is particularly good for medium-size gapers. Most areas are accessible by foot on a minus 1 foot or better tide.

Crabbing is good throughout the year and they can be taken in all the channel areas during low or high tide.

All the necessary crabbing and clamming gear can be purchased or rented in Netarts or in nearby Tillamook. Campgrounds, restaurants, and motel accommodations all can be found in Netarts, nearby Oceanside, or in Tillamook. Two boat ramps are available in Netarts Bay. Boats can be rented in Netarts Bay.

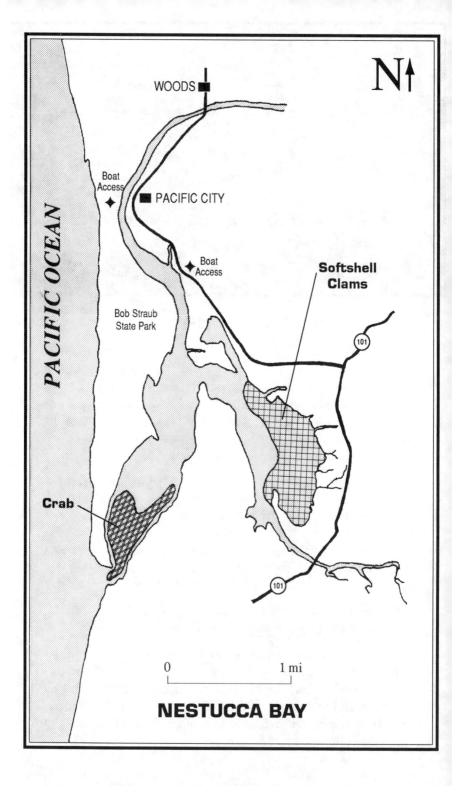

NESTUCCA BAY

NESTUCCA BAY

A relatively small bay on the central Oregon Coast, Nestucca Bay offers both crabing and soft shell clam digging opportunities. In addition to breathtaking scenery and virtually no development, the competition for clams and crabs from other sportsmen is quite low.

Nestucca Bay is only a short drive from I-5 and the Willamette Valley. It is about 20 miles south of Tillamook by Highway 101 or the Tierra Del Mar Road.

Softshell clams are found in the eastern lobe of this inverted V-shaped bay just below the mouth of the Little Nestucca River. It is not an extensive bed, however, adequate numbers exist to provide locals and tourists plenty of good eating. Any minus tide will expose these clam flats.

The crabbing in Nestucca Bay I'd rate as fair most of the year and very good in late summer and early fall. Best crabbing is found in the channels and deeper areas of the lower main bay.

All necessary supplies and accommodations are available in Pacific City as well as boat and motor rentals. There are three boat access points around the bay.

For a special treat observe the launching of the sport and commercial dory fishing fleet which occurs just north of Pacific City at Cape Kiwanda. During the summer months these brave fishermen actually launch their dories through the treacherous surf to gain access to excellent salmon fishing. This event has gained notority as a famous tourist attraction and is an exciting spectacle to behold.

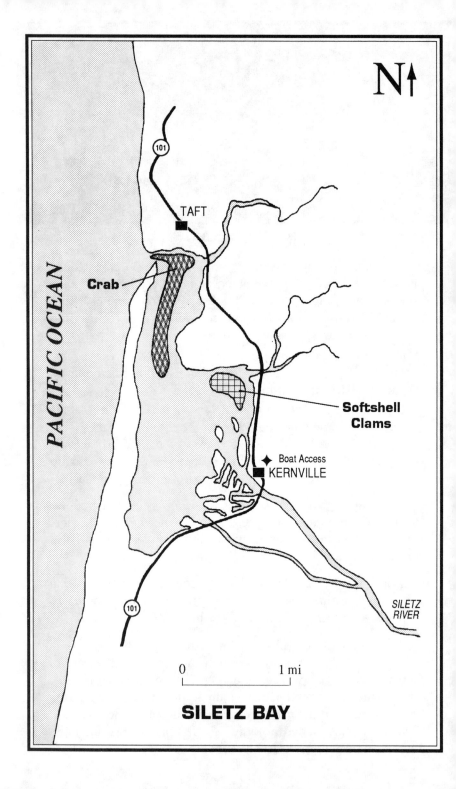

SILETZ BAY

SILETZ BAY

Siltez Bay is another picturesque and relatively small estuary situated on the central Oregon coast right along Highway 101 between Lincoln City and Newport. Much of the bay has silted in over the years and has created some fair clam digging among the hundreds of birch-white stumps and snags that have settled in the mud.

The only clam species available for sport harvest in Siletz Bay is the eastern softshell. Reasonable numbers of them inhabit the flats between Cutler City and Kernville with best digging near the mouth of Drift Creek. Any near minus tide is enough to reveal these clam flats, however, digging is what I would call only fair.

The lower bay and its sandy shoreline is a very popular tourist attraction with excellent crabbing opportunities. Crabbing in this small bay is good at times although the competition between users can get intense. The channel area between Cutler City and Taft is where the majority of crabs are taken. August, September, and October are the best time to set out your pots or rings.

An abundance of motels, campgrounds, and restaurants are available in the surrounding area with Lincoln City to the north and Newport to the south. Bait and all the necessary clamming and crabbing equipment can be locally purchased from a variety of sport shops. A boat ramp, moorages, and boat rentals are available.

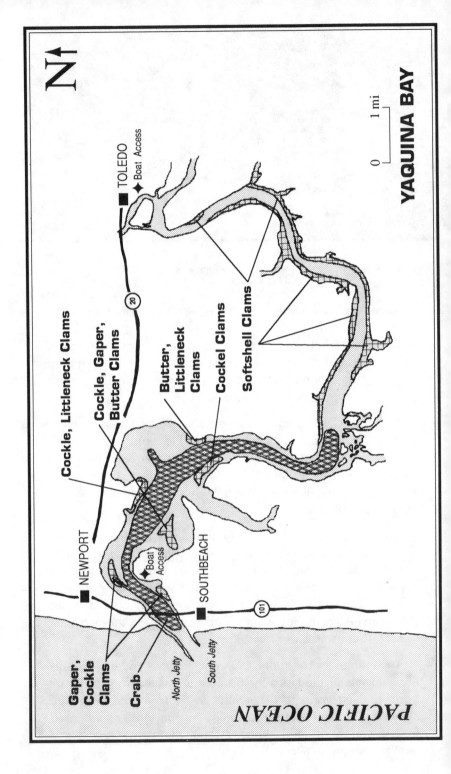

YAQUINA BAY

Centrally located along the Oregon coastline, Yaquina Bay is definitely near the top of the list in terms of excellent crabbing and clam digging opportunity and it is Oregon's fifth largest estuary. Surrounded by the very tourist-oriented town of Newport, it is accessed by Highway 101 on the coast and from the Willamette Valley and I-5 by Highway 20. It is about a two hour drive from either Portland or Eugene and only an hour away from the Corvallis-Albany area.

This important recreational estuary is a superb clam digging bay which offers a good variety of clams. The cockle clam contributes most of the sport catch followed by softshell and gaper clams; littleneck and butter clams are of minor consequence. Again, the lower more saline portions of the bay are where you will find excellent catches of gapers and cockles on minus tides. Softshells are abundant and found several miles up-bay between the town of Toledo and the Riverbend area near Pool Slough. Most any low tide is adequate for good softshell digging.

81

Crabbing is excellent year round and the deeper channel areas of the bay's lower three miles are the best. Talk to locals for the hot crabbing areas as locations change from season to season.

Yaquina Bay and the town of Newport are an outdoor vacationer's bonanza. No problem finding places to eat, sleep, and rent equipment here. The Port of Newport at South Beach has provided launching ramps, moorages, and public docks. A private ramp can be found at Idaho Point on the south side of the bay and a public ramp is located near Toldeo. All necessary equipment can be secured locally.

The marine enthusiasts can really enjoy themselves in Newport. It looks, smells, and sounds like a commercial fishing town. The Marine Science Center and the Undersea Gardens offer the visitor a unique educational experience in marine biology. I believe that the Yaquina Bay outdoor experience is one everyone should try at least once.

Fresh OYSTERS

Fresh Yaquina Bay Oysters are grown and harvested daily at Oregon's oldest oyster farm, founded in 1907.

Visit our Retail Store, located six miles up the Yaquina Bay Road from Newport, Oregon, for the freshest, year 'round selection of oysters.

We feature the following fresh items:

WE'RE EASY TO FIND:
6 miles east of Embarcadero on Yaquina Bay Road

- **Oysters in the Shell**
- **Oyster Meat**
- **Oyster Cocktails**
- **Smoked Oysters**
- **Steamer Clams**
- **and More!**

OREGON OYSTER FARMS — INC. —

Open 7 days a week from
9:00 AM 'til 5:00 PM

6878 Yaquina Bay Road
P.O. Box 2151
Newport, Oregon 97365
(541) 265-5078
fax (541) 265-2401
OregonOyster@actionnet.net

WE SHIP OYSTERS WORLDWIDE... JUST ASK!

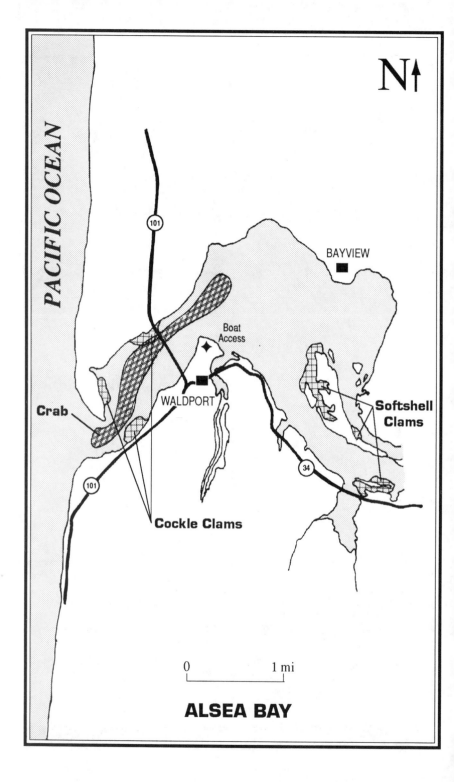

PACIFIC OCEAN

N

BAYVIEW

Boat
Access

WALDPORT

101

101

34

Crab

Cockle Clams

Softshell
Clams

0   1 mi

ALSEA BAY

ALSEA BAY

Alsea Bay is another medium-sized coastal estuary that will provide a delightful crabbing and clam digging experience. It is situated along Highway 101 about 15 miles south of Newport and only an hour's drive from Corvallis and the Willamette Valley by Highway 34.

The lower bay is great for raking cockles because it is almost pure sand with little debris, mud and gravel. Cockles are present in good numbers on the flat below the town of Waldport. The most popular cockle fishery is in water three to four feet deep at a minus 2.0 tide level below the Bayshore Motel. Clammers using specially made long-tined rakes and wetsuits do well in this area. Diggers can also find a few gaper clams along the southern and northern shorelines below the bridge. A good softshell bed exists on the southern shore just east of Eckman Slough. This flat is exposed on any near minus tide.

This is one of the better crabbing bays. Most crabs are boated in the channel below Lint Slough. Crabbing is best the closer you are to the mouth but be very careful, there are no jetties and the surf is dangerously close! Non boaters catch good numbers of crab off the port docks in downtown Waldport.

The city of Waldport has several motels and developed campgrounds are nearby. All needed equipment can be purchased locally. There are several moorages along the bay and boats may be rented.

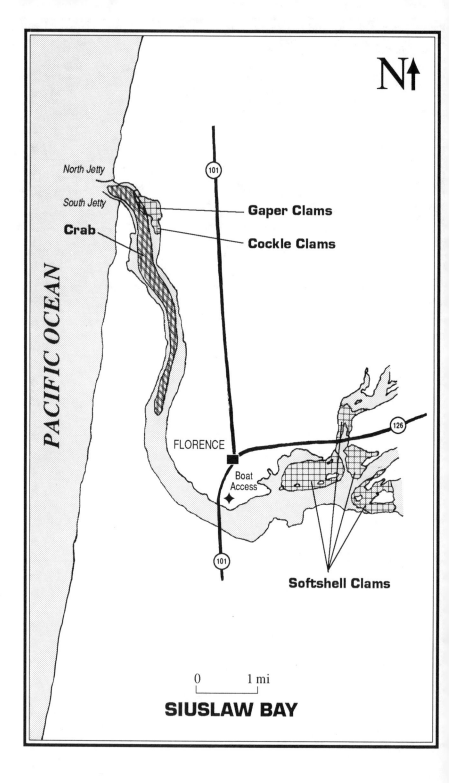

SIUSLAW BAY

SIUSLAW BAY

Siuslaw Bay is a medium-sized estuary that has fine crabbing and softshell clam digging and is only a one hour drive from the Willamette Valley and Eugene by Highway 126. One hour north on Highway 101 is Newport. Surrounded by mountain-like ivory sand dunes, this long and slender bay is a site to behold.

Although a few cockles and a rare gaper clam are occasionally taken by sport diggers in the lower bay near the mouth, Siuslaw Bay is well known for its excellent softshell clam flats located on both sides of the bay between Florence and Cushman. Clams are quite abundant and have a reputation for large average size. Any reasonably low tide will expose at least part of these excellent clam flats.

Crabbing is consistently good from April through October or until the first major rains. Best crabbing is in the lower channel from the Coast Guard station to the jetties. A large pier is situated near the beginning of the South Jetty where non-boaters can try their hand at crabbing with good chances for success.

The quaint little bay town of Florence has everything you need in the way of supplies, campgrounds, excellent restaurants and motels. The downtown waterfront area is unique and entertaining to say the least! Boat rentals and moorages are available, however, only one ramp currently services the entire lower bay and is located near downtown Florence.

ON THE RIVER
IN OLD TOWN FLORENCE
RV PARK
& MARINA

541-997-3040
1ST & HARBOR • P.O. BOX 1638
FLORENCE, OREGON 97439

LOCATED ON THE CENTRAL OREGON COAST... the Port of Siuslaw's RV Park is adjacent to the Siuslaw River at 1st & Harbor Streets, in Florence, a quiet coastal town of 6200.

The park has 85 sites: 59 spaces with full hookups and 26 spaces with water & electric hookups. All sites include basic cable tv connections.

Moorage facilities are also available. Check with the RV park office on reserving a slip.

Nestled in Old Town, away from the busy highways, the park offers in-town conveniences with an "off the beaten path" setting.

Include us in your travel plans...call today to make reservations!

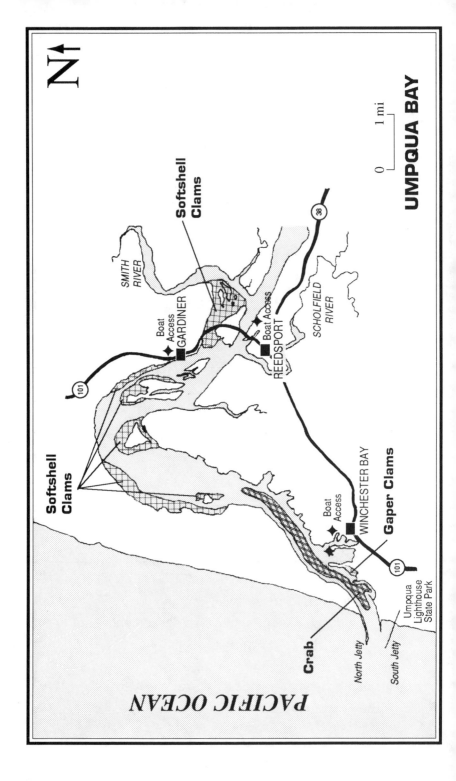

UMPQUA BAY

UMPQUA BAY

No finer outdoor recreational experience can be found in Oregon that compares to a summer's afternoon spent clam digging and crabbing on Umpqua Bay, the Beaver State's third largest estuary. Anyone that knows me personally might consider this a totally biased statement since I have lived near and worked on this bay for the past 12 years. Biased I am, but the statement still stands.

Except for the blemish of a large paper mill built at Gardiner on the upper end of the bay, this estuary is virtually undeveloped and near pristine. Crabs and softshell clams are plentiful and majestic sand dunes and towering evergreens surround the bay. Swans, eagles, and playful seals are routine sights. And to top it all off, competition from other crabbers and clammers is only modest at best.

Umpqua Bay is located 1/2 hour north of Coos Bay and south of Florence and only a one hour drive from Roseburg or Cottage Grove. It is accessed by Highway 101 on the coast and Highway 38 to I-5 and the valley.

With the exception of a small population of gaper clams found near the jetties and the Old Coast Guard Pier, softshell are the most important recreational clam in the Umpqua. This long and narrow estuary may well have the largest population of "mud clams" in Oregon with the largest average size. Softshells will average a full 1/2 pound and larger in certain parts of the bay. Good softshell digging begins about one mile up river from Winchester Bay and large numbers are found a mile or more above the town of Gardiner. A boat is needed to reach most clam flats, however, the beach in front of Gardiner and the mud flats at the mouth of Smith River below Highway 101 get heavy use from non-boaters. Clams in this area are somewhat smaller because of this heavy use. A few excellent softshell areas for boaters are: the northern end of Steamboat Island, The Point, and the Army Hill mud flats. Any .5 low tide or better will reveal most softshell beds in the Umpqua.

A few razor clams are found in the surf near the North Jetty and the gapers found in the lower bay can be taken with a minus 1.5 or lower tide.

Salmon Harbor

Located In Beautiful Winchester Bay

Fish the Umpqua River

Crab Off the Docks

Tell your friends...

...Come visit Salmon Harbor Marina and RV in Winchester Bay for boating and recreation that is simply the best on the Oregon Coast. Salmon Harbor Marina and RV has 900 boat slips with water and electricity.

Additional facilities include 300 RV camp sites on the water with access to the docks, restrooms, and showers. Two boat launch ramps for the day users with a lot of parking. There's also getting to be more and more shopping opportunities each month at Salmon Harbor. Our friendly, courteous staff looks forward to helping you.

Remember:
The Fun Starts in Reedsport-Winchester Bay
Call 503-271-3407

Crabbing in the lower Umpqua near Winchester Bay is one of the Oregon coast's best kept secrets. People are just beginning to discover how good the crab fishing really is. The merchants of Winchester Bay annually sponsor a cash contest to capture "Cleo" the tagged crab which attracts hundreds of hopefuls each summer. Crabbing is best in the lower two miles of the bay in the channel areas. The river channel opposite Winchester Bay is one of the better locations for consistent catches. The Social Security Beach Cove below the Old Coast Guard Pier is also quite popular. The Old Coast Guard Pier gets heavy use by non-boaters. Crabs can also be captured off the floating docks in Winchester Bay during the summer months. Good crabbing begins in the spring, gets excellent in August and September and can last until November or December depending on how heavy the winter rains are.

Plenty of motels and campgrounds are present in the area and five boat ramps have been developed around the bay. Crabbing and clamming equipment can be bought or rented in Reedsport and Winchester Bay. Lots of moorage space is found in Winchester Bay however, no boat rentals are available at this writing.

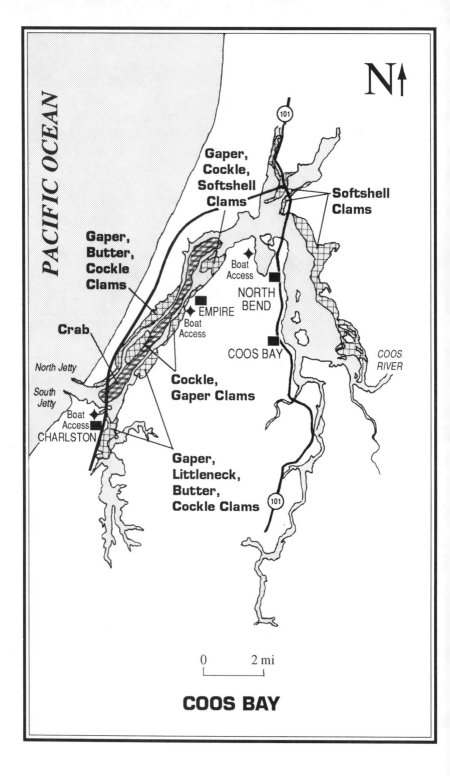

COOS BAY

photo by Ward Robertson

COOS BAY

Coos Bay is the largest estuary in Oregon outside of the Columbia River. Many people agree that it has the finest crabbing and clam digging found anywhere in Oregon. Coos Bay is a 1/2 hour drive south of Reedsport and Umpqua Bay along Highway 101, two hours from Eugene via Highway 38, and a four hour drive from Portland. Although this bay is fairly well developed and is a deep-draft port with large ships passing in and out, all species of clams are found in abundance and crabbing is superb nearly all year long.

The lower bay is loaded with cockles, butter clams, and gapers. Littlenecks or steamers are more abundant than in most other bays, but still they are only a small part of the total sport harvest. Popular digging areas for these species are the Charleston and South Slough mud flats, Pigeon Point, Clam Island and the North Spit. Any good minus tide will expose these areas. A couple of isolated populations of razors are found low in the bay near Charleston but tides must be extremely low and success is only fair.

The upper bay east and west of Highway 101 has some excellent softshell beds and is a fairly popular digging area. Scattered pockets of clams are found all over the upper bay, however, the flats north and south of the Menasha Dike

Road, which leads from Highway 101 to the North Spit, produces the bulk of the softshells dugs in Coos Bay. Diggers should be aware that a privately owned oyster bed is located in this area and sport harvest is illegal. A .5 or lower tide is fine for harvest of softshells in this area.

Crabbing in Coos Bay is about as good as it gets. I have never failed to bring home good numbers of both Dungeness and red rock crabs each and every time I have tried crabbing in Coos Bay. Set your traps or rings in the main channel between Empire and Charleston about one hour each side of high or low tide and you will get crabs. A real bonus is that a large number of red rock crabs are found in this estuary and the limit is 24 with no size or sex restrictions. These super hard-shelled crabs have excellent flavored meat and they often make up over fifty percent of the total catch.

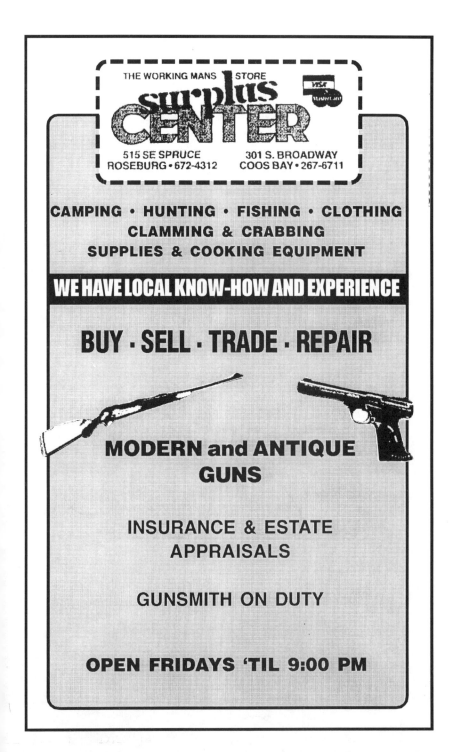

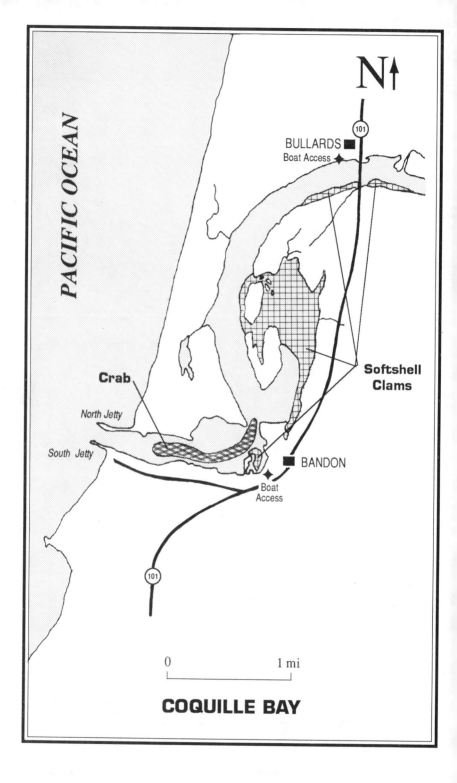

N

PACIFIC OCEAN

101

BULLARDS ■
Boat Access ◆

Crab

North Jetty

**Softshell
Clams**

South Jetty

■ BANDON
Boat
Access ◆

101

0   1 mi

COQUILLE BAY

COQUILLE BAY

The Coquille River estuary is the southern most bay in Oregon where clams and crabs are present in catchable numbers. It is long and very narrow with relatively little development and practically no competition from other sportsmen.

Coquille Bay is a full 2-1/2 hour drive from Eugene, 1-3/4 hours from Roseburg via Highway 42, and 1/2 hour south of Coos Bay along Highway 101.

When you say you are going clam digging in Coquille Bay that means eastern softshells. A good population exists and the best areas are just up-bay from the town of Bandon near the treatment plant, along the north bay 1/2 mile or so up-bay from Bandon, and there is a small bed along the south jetty. A .5 or better low tide is adequate for good softshell digging.

Crabbing in Coquille Bay is good from May through October. Most of the catches occur in the main channel from the jetty jaws to a mile or so above Bandon. The Bandon city docks are a good place to crab for non-boaters. Boat ramps are located at Bullards Beach State Park near Highway 101 and at Bandon.

Restaurants, motels and sport shops are plentiful in Bandon. This coastal town is a tourist's dream come true. It has a quaint little fishing harboi, a sternwheeler for scenic bay tours, lots of gift shops, and spectacular scenery.

Our ocean and the Coquille River are gifts. As kind caretakers of these waters, we can save a little for the next generation. Knowing is a start.

- 50 species of seabirds eat plastics, feel full and starve
- Debris from merchant ships amounts to 5,710,000 tons in our oceans annually
- An estimated 50,000 fur seals die each year due to entanglement in marine debris.

Twenty-seven countries now agree it's illegal to throw plastics into our oceans. More and more people care.

Thanks for your help.

THE PORT OF BANDON

CONVENIENT ORDER FORM

YES! I want to order more copies of this book at $9.95 (include $1.00 postage per book). Discount 10% if ordering two to five books. Discount 20% if ordering six or more books. Please allow two weeks for delivery. Thanks.

NAME _____

ADDRESS _____

CITY _____ **STATE** _____ **ZIP** _____

Number of books being ordered _____

TOTAL AMOUNT ENCLOSED
(Check or Money Order) $_____

Mail to: **Adventure North Publishing, Co.**
                P.O. Box 1601
                Waldport, Oregon, 97394
                (503) 563-3743

Adventure North Publishing also publishes *"Clam Digging and Crabbing in California", "Clam Digging and Crabbing in Washington" and "Oregon Hunting Guide".* For more information, write or call the publisher listed above.